Matthew was born on the island of Tasmania, to a hard-working family in a rural community. As an active young sportsman, he overcame a chronic hip injury which affected his quality of life for 6 years. After graduating from University, he started his professional career in several global commodity trading houses. After fulfilling a 7-year plan, he then embarked on what would eventually become almost 4 years of solo backpacking around the world.

LIFE LESSONS FOR ADULTS

A BOOK ABOUT EMBRACING CHANGE & FINDING BALANCE

Copyright © Matthew James Dyer Dornauf 2021

978-0-646-83564-8

To all the people who

taught me these lessons,

I love you all.

THE
JOURNEY SO FAR

Goal Setting	8
Money	17
Making Massive Change	23
The Fear of the Unknown	31
Friendships	38
Being Present	47
Relationships	54
Mistakes	72
Leadership	88
Making Growth a Habit	99
Finding Balance	105
Lessons for the Future	112

All personal goals begin

life as ideas in our

imagination

EMBRACING CHANGE

If you don't quantify your goals, then your mind is where they will remain

FINDING BALANCE

Writing down your goals

is the first step towards

"doing" them

EMBRACING CHANGE

Break your goals down into a series of much smaller and obtainable steps, rather than one giant leap

FINDING BALANCE

You must be prepared to

learn along the path to

your goals

EMBRACING CHANGE

If you do not come up with a

plan for your life, then someone

will do it for you

FINDING BALANCE

If you don't ask, then the

answer will always be no

EMBRACING CHANGE

Many things in life are satisfying

because they are difficult

FINDING BALANCE

If you quit too soon you

may miss the lesson

EMBRACING CHANGE

Do not expect to learn

everything you need to know

about money from your parents

FINDING BALANCE

To live outside your means, is to live a life enslaved by money

EMBRACING CHANGE

When working towards a financial goal, make sure you have a clear end point and that you stick to it

FINDING BALANCE

If you are successful, then there will eventually come a time when money is not the most important thing in your life

EMBRACING CHANGE

The more you consume, the harder you have to work

FINDING BALANCE

Happiness is a lot less

expensive than sadness

EMBRACING CHANGE

When unpleasantness lingers, it's normally a sign that you need to get up and change something

FINDING BALANCE

You will never know what

is good or bad, or what

you do or don't like until

you've tried both

EMBRACING CHANGE

The more things you try, the more opportunities you create

FINDING BALANCE

From a young age, we are asked: "What do you want to do for the rest of your life?". In reality, life is a series of much smaller decisions, that eventually lead you to do more of what you do like and less of what you don't like.

EMBRACING CHANGE

To live is to experience things,

not sit around pondering the

meaning of life

FINDING BALANCE

It is possible for 1 person

to be right and 9 people

to be wrong

EMBRACING CHANGE

You never lose the ability to control what's happening in your life

FINDING BALANCE

The perception of "not having enough time" is a direct result of your priorities

EMBRACING CHANGE

Grow comfortable with being outside your comfort zone

FINDING BALANCE

You will never learn more

than the moment you

are outside of your

comfort zone

EMBRACING CHANGE

Upon deciding to do something challenging, it is important to push through the initial stage of regret

FINDING BALANCE

You're not going to die

EMBRACING CHANGE

The worst case scenario is very

rarely the most likely

FINDING BALANCE

There is a difference between rational and irrational fear. Rational fear is not wishing to step into a cage with a lion. Irrational fear is being fearful of something simply because you've never done it before

EMBRACING CHANGE

Eventually you will come to know "The Fear of the Unknown" by another name...

FINDING BALANCE

Make the most of all

your connections

EMBRACING CHANGE

Friends are your support

network and source of

fresh perspective

FINDING BALANCE

Surround yourself with people who will preserve your mindset, not destroy it

EMBRACING CHANGE

Talk and interact with people

face to face

FINDING BALANCE

There is gold in every connection, even the non romantic ones

EMBRACING CHANGE

An over-reliance on technology prevents the development of our human traits

FINDING BALANCE

If first you give,

you will receive

EMBRACING CHANGE

Enemies mean energy

FINDING BALANCE

Don't judge people,

talk to them

EMBRACING CHANGE

Focus on the beauty and fun of

the journey, rather than where

you are headed

FINDING BALANCE

One of the best ways to

live in the moment is to

not make any plans at all,

just go with the flow

EMBRACING CHANGE

Let some things play out,

rather than overthinking

them too much

FINDING BALANCE

Let others set your bearing

EMBRACING CHANGE

When you're moving towards a

destination, it's very important

to pay attention to the road

FINDING BALANCE

There is no place like here,

there is no time like now

EMBRACING CHANGE

Immerse yourself in nature

FINDING BALANCE

Lasting love is finding

someone who loves you

equally back

EMBRACING CHANGE

Everyone wants to feel wanted

and special, not just you

FINDING BALANCE

Love should be cherished,

but if you hold on too

tightly you may run the

risk of smothering it

EMBRACING CHANGE

True love allows each person to

follow their own path

FINDING BALANCE

Some relationships progress with children, some by starting a business together, some with a house, some with a dog, some by moving closer to family, some with more travel, some with a change of career...

EMBRACING CHANGE

Listen to your partner

FINDING BALANCE

What kills a relationship

is precisely the lack of a

challenge, the feeling that

nothing is new anymore

EMBRACING CHANGE

Keep your little romantic

routines with your partner

FINDING BALANCE

A cuddle doesn't

always have to turn into

something physical

EMBRACING CHANGE

Take pleasure in getting each other in the mood for something physical. It will determine the intensity of what follows

FINDING BALANCE

Don't ever try to change anything about your partner or your friends. Accept them as you first met them

EMBRACING CHANGE

Discuss with your partner what each other needs for themselves to be happy and support each other's dreams

FINDING BALANCE

It is very important to talk whilst building the perfect intimacy

EMBRACING CHANGE

Continue to look, feel and dress your best for your partner (be proud that your partner is attracted to you and you to them)

If you want a romantic connection to grow into something more then it can be your only romantic connection and you need to physically see each other

EMBRACING CHANGE

Connections mean that you

are unique to each other

in the world

FINDING BALANCE

To build a long term connection, you need time and space to gradually fit your lives together

EMBRACING CHANGE

If you want a serious relationship, then you need to slow things down a bit and savour the moment

FINDING BALANCE

Mistakes cause evolution,

never be afraid

of mistakes

EMBRACING CHANGE

We are all walking through life for the first time. We will continue to make mistakes and learn from them

FINDING BALANCE

Give new experiences

time but pick up on

the signs

EMBRACING CHANGE

Intelligence is understanding you are in a crisis, then doing something about it

FINDING BALANCE

It's important to recognise that there is a difference between good and bad pain

EMBRACING CHANGE

Listen to your mind and body.

If bad pain lingers, you need to

change what you're doing

In time you will realise why

you weren't right for

each other

EMBRACING CHANGE

The moment you choose to stop learning is the moment you begin to fight change

FINDING BALANCE

Constant new experiences

can be unhealthy

EMBRACING CHANGE

If you are tiring of someone just

add more people to the mix,

don't ditch them

FINDING BALANCE

Whilst voicing a grievance,

take into consideration

the land in which

you stand

EMBRACING CHANGE

Boredom and over stimulation

are routes to unhappiness

FINDING BALANCE

It is important to know

your faults but also

your qualities

EMBRACING CHANGE

If you don't do it, then maybe

nobody will

FINDING BALANCE

There are no solutions

down the path to self pity

EMBRACING CHANGE

Don't focus on being the perfect human, instead there comes a point when you should focus on being the best version of yourself

FINDING BALANCE

The best teachers will

always be students

EMBRACING CHANGE

Be patient, let people learn

and make the same mistakes

you did

FINDING BALANCE

When giving advice,

remove yourself from

the situation

EMBRACING CHANGE

Everybody's different

FINDING BALANCE

A student must eventually

be sent off to gain

experience of their own

EMBRACING CHANGE

Sometimes you need to be

tactful when righting

an injustice

FINDING BALANCE

Not everyone will want

your help

EMBRACING CHANGE

It is much better to teach than

to tell or provide

FINDING BALANCE

There is more in all of us

EMBRACING CHANGE

Skills can only be mastered

through practise

Every person has the

ability to learn more than

they realise

EMBRACING CHANGE

One whetstone must eventually

be replaced by another

FINDING BALANCE

Grow, simplify, relax, grow

simplify, relax....

EMBRACING CHANGE

Trust your gut and trust you are

on the right path

FINDING BALANCE

Life is like riding a bicycle,

to keep your balance

you must keep

moving forward

EMBRACING CHANGE

Organisation cannot be sustained. Keep dreaming and doing

FINDING BALANCE

A builder must keep

on building

EMBRACING CHANGE

You need a combination of me time, partner time and friend time for the ultimate balance

FINDING BALANCE

You can't have the same experiences again, you can only have new experiences

EMBRACING CHANGE

Eating a healthy balanced diet wasn't meant exclusively for childhood

FINDING BALANCE

Keep exercising regularly

Helping people is as good a serotonin regulator as exercise

FINDING BALANCE

Take pride in your

appearance

EMBRACING CHANGE

Do what makes you happy but

don't be selfish

FINDING BALANCE

Be yourself, be nice

EMBRACING CHANGE

Never betray your morals

FINDING BALANCE

In order to have faith in

your own path, you need

not prove that someone

else's is wrong

Love openly and in the manner

you wish for the future of

the world

FINDING BALANCE

There is no sanctuary of

virtue like home

EMBRACING CHANGE

Share your knowledge

with others

FINDING BALANCE

SPECIAL
THANKS TO

Renske Rombouts & My Family, Marc Ackermann, Egal Gabay, Sarah De Gouw, Nicola Tuckey, Dan Blackwell, Michael Jones, Georgia Hubert, Cobham 612, Outward Bound New Zealand, Vinnie Scavone, Amber McBride, Fabio Carlucci, Luciano Barros, Charlie Smith, Pakamon Engchuan, Lucie Heyworth, Hina Raja, Lantern House Backpackers, Mahdi Khan, Geordie White, Oliver Farchim, Daniel Ward, Joel Åckerland, Laura Kakko, Happy House Backpackers, Max Kejroth, Roberto Santillan, Kumar Bhattacharyya, Enrique Velazco, Lawrence Cobuccio, Mad Monkey Koh Rong Samloem, Maddison Hunter, Robert Ante Roncevic, Sankee Gath, Sidath Dharmapala, Adam Binford, Holly Bougourd, Paulo Coelho, Ben McLennan, Vanda Niemeyer, Antonia Antoni Mensch, Pajamas Koh Chang, Lisa Liebisch, Daniel Hawkes, Emma Jarvis, Tom Green, Steven Cuthbert, St Hilda's College, Native Design Agency

www.ingramcontent.com/pod-product-compliance
Lightning Source LLC
LaVergne TN
LVHW051601080426
835510LV00020B/3079